The Beginning of the Fields

The *Beginning* of the Fields

Angela Shaw

TUPELO PRESS
North Adams, Massachusetts

COVER AND TEXT DESIGN BY HOWARD KLEIN.

First paperback edition May 2009

Printed in Canada.

Tupelo Press
P.O. Box 1767
Eclipse Mill, 243 Union Street, Loft 305
North Adams, Massachusetts 01247
Telephone: (413) 664-9611/Fax: (413) 664-9711
editor@tupelopress.org/www.tupelopress.org

Tupelo Press is an award-winning independent literary press that publishes fine
fiction, non-fiction and poetry in books that are a joy to hold as well as read. Tupelo
Press is a registered 501(c)3 non-profit organization and relies on donations to carry
out a mission of publishing extraordinary work that may be outside the realm of the
large commercial publishers.

 Supported in part by an award from the National Endowment for the Arts

NATIONAL
ENDOWMENT
FOR THE ARTS

For my parents,
William and Linda Shaw

Contents

IV

V   Five Fences: On Marrriage

I

Wheat

i.

Someone has made something of the day.
In the strain of noon, in the green marriage
between wheat and sky, someone has gone
traceless into the white farmhouse. Someone's
left the landscape in furious repose.

ii.

The wheat would eat everything.
Like the tide come in, it floods the fields
and reaches for the eaves of the olive-
drab outbuildings, its gold a single note
held the entire measure of July.

iii.

Half the work is waiting. The sky is pure
hesitance, a cloudless trance. Its shyness
bears down tenderly on the wheat,
the thing that seems like silence trapped
in its body of blue currency.

iv.

Devoted tracts of blue and gold like lapses
of time in which work disburdens the mind
of thought. In between them live the wind-
spent trees, the complicated minutes.
Beyond is the sea, eking out its living.

Children in a Field

They don't wade in so much as they are taken.
Deep in the day, in the deep of the field,
every current in the grasses whispers *hurry*
hurry, every yellow spreads its perfume
like a rumor, impelling them further on.
It is the way of girls. It is the sway
of their dresses in the summer trance-
light, their bare calves already far-gone
in green. What songs will they follow?
Whatever the wood warbles, whatever storm
or harm the border promises, whatever
calm. Let them go. Let them go traceless
through the high grass and into the willow-
blur, traceless across the lean blue glint
of the river, to the long dark bodies
of the conifers, and over the welcoming
threshold of nightfall.

The Beginning of the Fields

It has been so easy to keep still,
out here where the dreaming
fields begin and the slow roads boil
to ghost. Everything is small
against a wall of heat: the sun's hole
closing in a blaze of beige,
melting and irrelevant, the far trees
crouching at the meadow's edge.
It has been easy. Is it what they call
a deadening, this place where no growth
goes too long unwatched? In a moment
the grasses will repeal that lone car's rush,
cicadas will take up their rush of song.
Listen, listen, listen. From insistence
they make a distant rain—*voice*
of the bridegroom, voice of the bride—
from the strain of waiting they weave
the dreaming fields. So long buried
how to begin? So long buried
what trouble swells the now-
forgotten farmhouse where *to dwell*
has meant forever *to deceive?*

II

Courtesan

The air grows thin. The men are less bewitched
of late, no longer appeased with flagrant
dessert set aflame, nor wowed by shellacked
tenacity of my coiffure. Tumid
and ruthless, they loosen the latitude
round their middles, visibly bored. Someone's
perfume, they sense, glided through here, fragrant
and vacant. I dull like silver. My jokes
mold. The little dinner party's carnage:
thick, residual soup puddled in low
bowls, pumice-rough edges of bread, sottish
remnants of rum-laced cake. Now the onset
of sweet, swift red wine headache, my face
still stiff where I fit my simper. The plaster
holds though cold aspic un-gels and candles'
drip hardens to sculpture. In the sofa's
leather the dim imprints visitors leave—
buttocks and thigh—turn vaguely lurid. Sad
ghosts of my lashes on scented tissue:
delicate mascara moth wings. Life pools
in the shallows. Later, unlaced, what breathes
in slip and stocking feet. Left to settle
what rich, indecent cream resurfaces.

Small Pleasures

The Wurlitzer stirs, all girl, all groan
and moment, everything pretty
hesitance

and pregnancy. Little furls
of lipstick, little wiles, sausage
curls beguile the makeshift

dusk, the boys, their pretty head-
over-heels makeshift liftoff.
Laughter curdles in the throats

and limbs of late-
April magnolia. A tree full of pink
wishes, each bud clenched

in its private
tantrum. Other petals spin
a tarantella: kleenexes

and kleenexes dropped in approximate
ladylike gesture.
On a high stool a lady or high

school girl tipples and swithers,
all purr and murmur, working
her clumsy rosary of car

keys and house keys, making the dim
room do her fast
dancing. Elsewhere cypriniform

fishes suck at the rough
creek bottom, muttering
leftovers, leftovers.

In the backwater Catholic
pucelles swelter
in their lycra-spandex Sunday

dresses,
all prayer and murmur, lip-
synching *my soul*

is thirsty for you O Lord,
and the bored organist kindles his bored
organ

for the misses, dizzy
with Jesus and little visions
of their own late-night

acts of mercy. The brimstone
boy, his mason jar full of snarling
bees, wades into the soft-core

porn of moths where they wallow
and dissolve in the dogbane,
knees and faces

glazed with pollen.
Nightly birdsong,
boozy

and uvular, suggests the indelicate
question
would she let her Texas

blues infect my red,
her wily
silences potent as jukebox

promises
in the low
dusk of the bowling alley

where the Wurlitzer
stirs, all girl, letting Motown
down easy.

West Virginia Spring

Ramps *stink worse than what wild
onion does*, but what is merely
unearthed is not

dirty. A wild leek, a lily. A furtive
girlhood spent tramping
through woods, unwinding

the skein of the heart like stolen
evidence. A pink
lipstick driven to its quick, in time,

nylons, the wayward
names of town boys, swollen
on the tongue and scarred

across catalpa bark. *They ain't
for ladies or for those
who court them.* The outer skin

around the bulb peeled back, the last
of delicate April
lifted like a fingerprint.

Crepuscule

Yellows cast their spells: the evening primrose
shudders unclosed, sells itself to the sphinx
moth's length of tongue. Again a lackluster
husband doesn't show. A little missus

eases the burnt suffering of a cat-
fish supper, undresses, slowly lowers
into a lukewarm tub. In her honeymoon
nightgown she rolls her own from the blue

can of Bugler, her lust a lamp the wick
of which is dipped in sloe gin. Hands
wander to her hangdog breasts, jaded Friday night
underpants, hackneyed nylon in heat.

Now his black taxidermy out-stares her, the stern
heads of squirrel and deer. Now the house confesses,
discloses her like a rumor, vague and misquoted.
From the porch, from the glider she spies rose-

pink twilight flyers—sphinx moths drinking
the calyx, the corolla, the stamen
dry. The stuttering wings, the spread petals
suggest an interlingual breathing, a beating

back of all false tongues. She thinks of the chaw
lodged in his lip when he talks or her husband's
middle finger in the snuff box and rubbed
along his gum. She walks, wanting him, into the latter-

math, into the primrose, the parched field itching
with critters. She walks, wanting and unwanting
him while birds miss curfew into the thick of the thigh-
high grass, craven and dangerous, in the heavy red.

The Closer You Get

to Leaving—the country
song I fashion, then unravel—
pines for a voice as nettled
as Loretta's, for fingers destined

to travel the guitar's fragile
neck, fretting his cheatin' steps from honky tonk
to home. *Ever since he left me*
takes lonesome for granted and downs

another of whatever Handsome's
pouring. Oh to languish in such rich
aftermath, such bathrobe-
till-happy-hour-hair-of-the-dog

extravagance. Instead, the closer
you get to leaving the quicker
I weave a web of whisper-
thin beginnings: *listless riverbank*

kiss, a drifting glimpse, now weeks
upstream from the closer you get
to *love*. The closer you hold me
the sooner *leaving* moves its gerund

feet, sleepwalking, shedding
like bedclothes the careless
pretense of a noun.
When I try to lay down

the requisite rails, the very lines
I cannot follow, my town
deletes itself from your horizon.
Leaving picks up steam, its engine

coughing fewer lost
goodbyes the smaller
I get from
gone.

Abandoned Church of Christ

The women should keep silence in the churches.
—I Corinthians 14:34

No song for the unseen
properties of the pond in winter, the particulars
of ice forming—discreet and mystery-

slickened—rim to middle. No song for silence
stealing gray-green over a body, freezing
the shallow

edges first, deepening, finally
meeting itself in the dead
center of a woman's

life. The voice turns
wordless, deciduous, shedding
the expendable, revealing

its newly unembellished
web of beckonings.
Who will come unto her *the question*

Who *the answer*.
The church disturbs its own
sleep, echoing stolen testament, an airtight

version of God's stale word
broken on this February
morning. No song for the defunct

potluck, the indifferent
husband grunted from bed,
the lowly gesture of her Sabbath

hair, coiled in easy recollection
of a girl's first
submission. What of the lopped

steeple, the deserted
churchyard, this marketed
property? The word gives rise

to eternal purchases, the compromise
of *flesh* for flesh. Now that prayer
inhabits every gesture, let her

ransom nothing. The hair
comes down, complies with the quiet
discipline of one hundred

nightly strokes. The throat
unfastened from her grandmother's
cameo, the slender throat unbuttoned

to his slightest touch—such
delight she finds in her own muted
seduction, the hidden

eucharist of her winter skin.
Beyond the long-standing
manse, the churchyard's wealth

of headstones, a row of thorn
apples grows
leeward. Stripped to its naked limbs

each articulates prevailing
wind, each a history, an anatomy
of implicit

come hithers and resistances.
Prayer inhabits every gesture.
What lost cause do they etch

across a paling backdrop?
Who would make of herself a new lodging
for his eloquent body? What she carried

to chapel, what they held—palpable
as an infant, as a flower—
can be born

everywhere, unfurling
in the February morning, disburdening
no song.

III

After Sleep the Wild Morning

glory's uninterrupted vine
describes a furtive turning on barbed

wire—the tendril tightening
like a python on its prey, disclosing

over and over the startled *oh* in *ownership*.
All night my body

held its tentative
place like a marker in the latest bedside

novel. Now I take up my life mid-
sentence—wending

syntax, drifting ellipses, the irresistible
punctuation of a sometime

lover. Nothing keeps. After sleep
I savor the morning's sweet

evictions: a disturbance
of warblers: silence conquered by

birdsong, birdsong
the eloquent pause wherein silence

takes its breath. After sleep this antique
question: How long can one live

within the body like a stale guest
room, stock-still, neat as a pin,

and unfrequented? In diffuse light, only
what is most profane, only what is holy

slowly opens: the long body
of work, the mouth

of the flower—song-valve—the latent
chamber closed to those I fear

would name me.
The embrace of the bindweed—

though graceless, some say—
speaks counterclockwise

volumes: *after sleep revise*
the wild morning, take to the necessary

hedges, the precious
wayside, take

hurtful possession of your vicious twisting
vine. Stumbling into thirty,

I become my own
prey, an utterance doubling

back on itself, entwined with the furtive
turning of the past. After sleep

the leaving road contrives
to keep me

slippery, drifting, ill-
defined. The convolvulous

dilates and acquires.
I live from myself like a suitcase.

Pornography

Painted, perfect, patient, I couch myself
in lace peignoir. I author the slouching hours
after dusk, bidding the sun go down
over Tucson or Memphis, conjuring love-
rooms from a little perfume, a little blues,
a little bourbon. Every romance opens
at the neckline. Every night a voluptuous
story line is teasingly unveiled, stocking
by stocking, exquisitely unfastened
at its climax. There are infinite methods
of table setting, of letting backdrop foretell
the spread, the dizzying lick of the graceful
fellatrix. A neatly banked fire is both action
and circumstance. I practice an interior
design, appointing the chamber with chance
reticence: the hush of a thick rug, the space
that embraces the furniture's curves. I rhyme
slipcover with pillow talk, the jaded wallpaper
with my eyes. My body lies to tell the truth,
each gesture disguised as stillness, each over-
wrought posed happening toward aftermath.
My past is strapless, hook-less, and eye-less.
I freelance, unlacing the vintage syntax
of seduction. My patron sated, I compose
myself—painted, perfect, patient as paper,
falling open like a book to my best parts.

Garden Party

Is that shirt flirting with you across the cotton
lawn? Not a shirt but a veritable whisper,
a sort of relaxed swagger, a seedy
allure. The man with the seersucker

ease is prone to softly silk-like talk, mellowed
stuff. You try a look that might provoke, a sally
in the opposite direction: cabanas at noon, the blues
of a slow-turning fan. Who would guess your underwire

disquiet, the half-life of your shelf-bra? Peacock-
mean in your fitted little half-body you
dazzle. The spare design of your butterfly
kiss passes as dress-up. Subdued, he harbors

a cooler-come-evening, loosened silhouette, a barbecue,
utterly unencumbered. A few graceful steps further
into the wilting summer. Plenty roomy. Down south:
a beautiful hang, an extra measure: you may just settle.

Blackberry Pie

The man my mother
takes to the barn
while I carve the other one
his second slice.

Thick-scented,
slick, peddling
Jesus or magazines.
How they come

to the door. Dumb
as full-blown
balloons and as thin-
skinned. Under

the eaves the spun
gray paper funnel sips
hornets
through its delicate

orifice. The nest she says
we leave out of pity.
The loose barn
letting go

a sharp-billed cry,
the way a jay's naked
call becomes his own
tormentor.

The pie ticking down.
Its vee spreads,
deepens, draws
untold black lace

houseflies. Strains
of her laughter. This boy
half listening, half-
cocked, necktie riding

his throat, dish licked
clean. What they back into—
unspeakable
sweetness,

her barn,
the staggering
buzz, what I wear
underneath.

Pin-up

Fabric is essence, a beckoning, an oddly
modulated charm. If swimsuits could talk
they might lightly, sweetly suggest August,

a week on the Gulf, dog days ever so finely
licked by the wind. An arresting cross-back
tank may insinuate the infinite, promise

button-down Fridays as fathomless as Dad's
gin glass and evenings nuanced by shades of silk
undress. Believe the French-cut, the string

bikini whose coy unloosings bespeak the sinuous
history of all that stays put. For the private collector
some choice specimens: luxurious shirtings

in the fixed groove of breakfast, a giddy contrivance
of pinstripes, sandwashed gauze against a tile-
blue sky, and—for barefoot betweentimes—virgin

denim suspended on a lush velvet lawn.
This is the must-have, the almost palpable
color of summer reverie: hibiscus, indigo, ginger, sweet

cream butter and wilted greens. Taste the hazy remnants
of your faded glories; breathe the mellowed
power of a good cigar. An abbreviated crimson

slipdress, a swatch of charmeuse laughter
from the patio is never beyond your grasp.
A mounted skirt allows a certain tension, a slick

and supple fusing, a double-breasted status
quo. In a thick-lidded languor the pinned things
dream of milkweed. Believe that hole-in-one feeling.

Heart

i.

Little fist, small tyrant, squat Napoleon
in drag, all day trying to punch your way out
of the wet bag of yourself.

ii.

Oh mutant, oh side show, diminutive
circus, you're a pure whirring
of auricles and ventricles—
all small belly and ear.
The better, you mutter, *to eat*
you with, to hear.

iii.

Author, bestseller, that slick
book you wrote's
a kick. Your finger's
on the pulse. You
are the essence,
the core
of it.

iv.

Sweet bungalow, cottage,
four-chambered flat of a kept
woman whose lover's gone
back to his wife. In these rooms

passion's over. The plush
thick of things pumps
past her.

v.

My gargoyle, dear sluice,
you let your own slow juices
trouble your chin, my beast, drooling
life's dinner.

vi.

Lost canal, timeworn Erie.
Iron and sugar and salt
speed through your locks,
and your valves
go like clockwork.
Even when this trade
route's stopped
who would dare
belittle it?

April

is all laze and boudoir. She reclines, wigless
and half-naked in the haze of her private
rooms, chain smoking, deflowering éclair
with furtive tongue, bemoaning the pinch
of her little miss shoes. She is more freckled
than is suspected, less young, and when the mouth
of her silk robe unfolds, it confesses
her dimpled skin, the lap of rich thigh
on rich thigh. She jiggles her clinky
bottles, sips at her tinctures, weeping
easily over this hidden toilette: burnt
curl, slipped hem, the short, huffy cough
of powder puff. Her muttered curses are coarse
as grosgrain as she totters in corset
and stockings, rehearsing protocol, her self-
mocking curtsy. But she clears like water and later
will deny you saw her or knew her as she
litters with lipstick imprints spring's cotillion.

Climbing Nightshade

Petals reflexed, purpled, obscuring
not one skinny pistil. All night I nurse

Joplin like a cordial, sipping bittersweet
piece of my heart, that throb

of song, draining her lush sad
gravel from the vacant

hours. Heartworn come October, I fall
in love with the word *concoction*, my latest

distillation gently extracted of your bootleg
laughter. *For you are the fruit of the vine, the work*

of human hands, my figment,
my abstraction. Every red not bled

from these feinting acres I capture
on my palette, talking with my mouth

still full of you, misconstruing for passion
the maple's crimson papers, the roadside's

rusty grasses. I stroke in off-color
tones what you cannot name: the livid

vein beneath the late corn—beige
and songless; apples now fattened, rotten, ill-

thought-of; bruised fruit, the notorious blonde
overdose, muted in the cheap spill

of newsreel; belladonna—lost girl-
lily toppling on her stalks. *All berries should be considered*

poisonous, all lost girls considered
distant from syntax, from marriage, from the well-laid

mortgaged brick. Now your night mind glances off
my body—autumn-ripe; the cherry-colored

berries *hang more gracefully over the river's*
brim than any pendant

in a lady's ear. Small wonder these leaves are heart-
shaped, that I take to wet places,

darkened gardens, falling in love
with the word. Bittersweet, climbing

nightshade, I work my groove till it's smooth
with sleep. I pull myself down tight. No lover

of color doesn't hover, moth-like: the right thought
applied to my petal-soft places. While *quell*

reads either *ease* or *kill*, nothing can hamper
my spelling you into this damp Louisiana

landscape, tracing with nimble finger the length
of the river, the pistil, each reflexed petal

left open just enough to the hoarse fall
dusk, just enough.

Striptease

She becomes her own encasement
and its foregone unlocking. Her dress—the safety
on a loaded gun. Her dress—a lessening
that she must seem to cleave. Her trained
momentum laced with static tactics—
that she may be the narrative and still
emerge its quivering, its silken heroine.
Her fever beads—a gilded sheath, chrysalid
ambivalence of skin disguised
as skin. Each successive ecdysis
teases her genius from its holster, each molting
a threshold she'll dress for, wearing
only ceremony and bearing herself over.

IV

Rear Window
after Grace Kelly

Love is a hovering, a deafening
batting of lashes. It presses

its lips to the opaque
blotting paper before breaking
and entering—a vision

suspended in moonlight, a museum

piece, a nude

summer hue. Love's petal-
starched dresses rustle in the under-
brush; its white cotton gloves

erase their own incriminating
traces. A lady

keeps her suitor guessing.

No matter the apparatus:
a handbag, a snifter, a pinch
in his drink,

a cinch

at the waist, an intellect trimmed
like a smart pillbox hat.
A lady proposes

a dangerous abetting
and proves her authenticity
by how easily

she bruises. Love is a cut-
up, a close-up,

a hovering.
This kiss is exquisitely
scripted and its twin

is terror.

Oyster

Your diffidence bewilders, sly miss of fire
hall dance. I spy you, mason, mending the place
between the wall and yourself, mum as a brick.
You are fastened, affixed, all mystery trapped
in your thin-lipped simper. Shy dear, what fear seals
you shut to the world's grit, its bad seed? You're no
rare beauty, and I am not what the mothers
have warned you against—some young bungler who pries
his way in, pilfers the gem, missing the rest.

Dear Men,

the world is not your urinal was worked
in intricate cursive on the wall of Dirty
Frank's unisex

john. For years I've fondled
that chiseled
syntax, rapt with its gracious

salutation, the sort of patience
reserved for grammar
school form

letters: *Dear Aunt Esther,*
How are you? we began, tracing
in graceful curves the pinned

etiquette of our careful
foremothers. Lazy in September
light, we acquired the hidden

privilege of *script*—a prefab
story for each girl to live in,
an elaborate split-

level gingerbread. And painstakingly,
because words were delicate:
I am fine. My hobbies

are Barbies and baton.
I imagine the anonymous
girl in that restroom taking the same

pains with her tired lips, applying
her latest dangerous shade, engaged
in the same curving precision, the same keeping

between the lines. To seem
fast she took her time, layered the wet
message on thick. Learning cursive, we spent

whole second grade weeks on a single
letter, lolling over pages of unfastened
capitals, mastering the Cleopatra-languid

L or the spit-curled O—
neat rows that mouthed our own
repetitive appetite, our blank surprise.

Where was she headed, that heartworn
girl? Miss Nelson forever
scolded us *walk—*

don't run but still chirped the virtues
of cursive. And, true, the smooth
letters sped one on

the other,
each on its way to the next better place,
the hipper situation. But we girls got nowhere

fast, dulling
our leads daily on the sanctioned
facts: *the cat had kittens,*

I'm going to be a flower girl in June.
Where was she headed—
slurred with gin, lipstick-slipped, in the half-

light of Dirty Frank's? What urgencies
spurred her straight to the ladylike?
First, her business, then this sly

reminder—*dear men*—benign
as a grocery list. Did her greeting
embrace a lover or traces

of lovers, a hoot
from a moving car, a boss, or a brute? I lately wonder
how a woman can put so fine

a point on her anger she can write
with it, how stumbling from the drunken
bar she can manage in three-inch

heels that strict
calligraphy, the compassion
that gathers in the private unisex

digression:
To Whom It May Concern:
I am fine.

Mobile Home

Out where the mail won't reach, itinerant
January tramples back in its thick
boots, unloads its burden of snow, stalling
geese on the water and pinning
someone's frail trailer to a lonely quarter
acre. Old, tested wrestling holds: winter's half-
nelson does in the tin shelter, brought
here from some Lubbock or Saginaw, bought
local. Staked to the yard two once-stray whelps
snarl their chains. Inside, a near-marriage sputters
and flares, left on a low burner. A pan
scorches. A warranty expires on the myth
of a fixity that courses forward.
Something persists, emerges: plastic dog
dish, orphan toys glow green, orange, inviolate
pink, poke through the snow, forced
corms, crocuses suspended midwinter.

Miscarriage

I go down to the roughhewn
field where the tiller's blade snagged
at the stubborn ground. I go down in the fresh-
turned soil, wet to my knees, and plant by feel
frail seedlings—Beefsteak and Better Boys.
I trowel a hole for each loose bundle
of roots, slosh water from my pail, and refill
the gap, my hands gathering at the base of each
fluid stem. I go down where my husband's long
shadow startles the grass. It is weeks
before we will again come carefully
unsewn, take to each other, hungry and thick-
tongued. I survey my row: a wicked stitch,
a wound to the ground I've inflicted
and mended, heedless, uneven, like a doped
line I might have walked in a scant hospital
gown. This evening each deeply toothed
leaf is mine. Even the spindly runts take
hold. I go down on all fours in search
of what I lost, something misplaced, like an heir-
loom scrap of antique lace, intricately clotted.
What will I say when she turns up at four
or six or ten, tangled and grass-stained, wet
to the knees. *You're late. Go wash.*
Go hunt the brush and bring me your fine head.

Obscure Persons

Before you are human you are nuance.
  You reach through the evening, the marshes,
    the parting. The beech dream their thick leaves
  sweet

with blood. How frugal the music
  of your pale green attachments, how greedy
    the syntax of your splitting into gills. *Little*

by little your whisper, your dictum.
  Little by little you thrive in the hull
    of my prior body, the wall between us

porous as coral, skeletal hedges
  frilled with feathery tentacles. Nightly
    the tentacles extend. Nightly the isolate

makes its disturbances, its beginnings
  gently obscured, furred over with leaf
    and pleasure. Now I'm doomed to grow

inevitable, doomed to a brute
  love, limnetic heaviness, to this parting
    of my mettle from my folly. The leaf forgets

its ethylene, its weathered speech, itself.
  The season's slow doses tug me under,
    the ache of a thousand shadow languages.

Bird Nests

The year dead-ends here. Clumsy December
stubs itself against its own rigid house-
keeping, spare and misaligned, nothing where
we remember it. Today a new word
grows into our easy speech: thermostat,
oatmeal, *tumor*, bedtime. Wise to the sun's
ruse we find laughable each half-assed try
at rising, at meridian. Now near
dusk we walk where the jagged lake grates
on the injured grass. Some sickness quickens
in you or what the doctors, those wordsmiths,
call *growth*. Beyond the house our great oak pumps
in the wind like a wild lung. Dumb earth.
The tap root's hit concrete and the sap won't
give. The evening sky silhouettes dark clots
of hair and straw, pilfered bits of thicket
caught in branches. Somebody lived here once.
Your x-ray haunts, the way they all badmouth
your chances, and the *spot* we're told to *watch
closely* like some rare species that may take
wing, flighty and blind, slowly spreading south.

Widower

Because it is unjust to leave the rampant
growth unchecked, I take my clippers to the hedge.
Under my vigilance, not one branch will edge
above the rest, not one slim slip of errant
grass escapes my mower's blade. My yard's well-kept,
but, more than that, it's fair: common weed and rare
bloom both plucked by my leveling hand. I dare
not rest. Grooming this lawn I've become adept
at meting justice. Still, the proud flowers rear
up. And I question the will of one who would
mow a good life down and leave me planted here.

Tango

Under the threat of timpani thunder he cuts
the rug: a plush, lizard-green shag, quivering
with bees and the stung throats of sweet
clover. Moreover, he is not yet dead.
His incessant metronome kicks
like an old guilt, and his footwork
still makes any stiff partner turn
silken. Drowsy, slow the mower rolls
its R's, some approximate concubine, undone
by the merciless choreography of late
August. What is left must be settled on.
His children have come, stilted and grown,
fingering their late mother's bone
china, unsettling dust in rooms thick with tinkling
figurines. A haunting of clocks crowds
his walls, each one holding its stale breath.
The afternoons drone on, stagy and dazed.
Dog-day cicadas exhume themselves, telegraph
their terrible passions from tree to tree.
Lacewings take wing from the uncut grass—
in time with his orchestrated back and forth—
and summer's last mow smells of red
wine or the first dark sex after
betrayal, then forgiveness.

The Improbable

August lingers, the improbable
scent of a lover thought
forgotten, brought now so easily

to the waking
surface. The late-
summer trees are stricken

with fruit.
Everywhere too much
accrues. For weeks the milkweed's

leaned toward my porch-
light, compiling its tight secrets,
its unripe

pods smiling shut
on my mouthless
wishes, on the infinite

kisses I count myself
to sleep by. Always the small
frailties we're handed, others'

boyhood paper routes,
their mill-working
grandfathers, their tender positions

for making love—can't
be handed back. Always
in the eyes of some

stranger a listening
so persistent I want to shed
in broad daylight, petal

by petal—ending
always on *he loves me*—the coy
design of my breathless

disguise. From fields, roadsides, waste
places, August stalks
me, talking

too much in muted tones
of my childhood, of the beauty
I was clearly

never meant to be.
All summer I spent
myself on this lavender

promise, set my watch
by the season's wild
growth, incautious and profligate

with how little
is left over of abundance.
Today someone has come to edit

the field—chicory, bull
thistle, goldenrod, and milkweed—
to a polite

stubble.
I'm told to hold so much
wildness, one learns first to tame

the improbable, to trim
the milkweed before its ready
pods indelicately

spread, sending adrift the exquisite grief
of silk and seed.
August fades, the stranger

becomes the intricate lover
I want but will likely never get
to slowly, most skillfully

unravel. Now in the leveled
field, I hear
the elaborate silence as his cadence

kindly regrets
that it cannot
embrace

my name.

V

Five Fences:
On Marriage

White Picket

The gown enters first—dazzling, embattled—
and then its bride on her cloud

of song. And if *the soul is a bride in a still place*,
then that place must be these silks

of perpetual waiting, layers of silence,
layers of patience. Not that it's the dress

she'll wear the rest of her life but that forever
she'll be taking it off, forever easing

her girlhood over her grown-up hair.
And the vow, too, is a comely boundary.

A fortress makes one worthy
of attack.

Barbed Wire

acre on acre
same joke same joke same
prickly mood come dusk prickly mood come dawn
     night provides
     a moment
     of opening animal
     tearings
            then mendings
soft across the sweet fields soft

Enceinte

every bit of her wilderness

subdued

Stone Wall

Walking the lonely
ridge, how easily we break
the graveyard's hush.

How steadily our own not-
talking mounts between us.
Here lie the calluses

that wouldn't soften,
a father's heart
hardened to a wayward

daughter, a neighbor's
grudge, a longing
spilled over like stolen well water—

precious—
a woman's winter dress
dark and wet with trespass.

Electric

Why did they come this far? The land an animal

they broke, rode bareback. The roadside beasts

adrift in dry obedience. No one can tell what holds

them. No witnesses here to the several riveting shades

of their fidelity. So few songs for how easy it is

to be faithful. *They have something to do with forever,*

the space behind the sky and the space behind the shadow.

Further and further, breathless, unbodied—

the circumference hums the threat of home.

Notes

Section I. Each of the three poems in this section was inspired by a Fairfield Porter painting of the same title. With thanks to Mary Ann Nichols.

page 10: "West Virginia Spring": Ramps are wild leeks native ro Apalachia. {Ramps} *stink worse than what wild onion does* and *They ain't for ladies or for those who court them* from *The Foxfire Book of Appalachian Cookery.*

page 13: "The Closer You Get": *Ever since he left me* from "I'm a Honky Tonk Girl" by Loretta Lynn.

pages 24 and 27: "Garden Party" and "Pin-up": Much of the language in these two poems was borrowed from J. Crew catalog copy.

page 32: " Climbing Nightshade": *All berries should be considered poisonous* from *How to Know the Wildflowers* by Mrs. William Starr Dana, and *hang more gracefully over the river's brim than any pendant in a lady's ear* from Henry David Thoreau.

page 54: "White Picket": *the soul is a bride in a still place* from "Berck-Plage" by Sylvia Plath.

page 58: "Electric": *They have something to do with forever, the space behind the sky and the space behind the shadow* from Anne Packard describing her own paintings, quoted in *New American Paintings: A Juried Exhibition in Print* (February, 1998).

Acknowledgments

Many thanks to the editors of the following journals in which these poems first appeared: *Bookpress*: "Tango"; *Carolina Quarterly*: "The Improbable"; *Chelsea*: "April," "Oyster," and "Courtesan"; *Field*: "Blackberry Pie" and "Rear Window"; *Indiana Review*: "Small Pleasures"; *Pleiades*: "Climbing Nightshade" and "Garden Party"; *Poetry*: "Children in a Field," "The Beginning of the Fields," "The Closer You Get," "Miscarriage," "Crepuscule," and "After Sleep the Wild Morning"; *Seneca Review*: "Abandoned Church of Christ," "Bird Nests," and "Pornography"; *Shankpainter*: "Dear Men," "Mobile Home," and "West Virginia Spring"; *Southern Poetry Review*: "Heart."

"Courtesan" was reprinted in *The Best American Poetry 1994*. "Crepuscule" was reprinted in *The Best American Poetry 1996*. "Pornography" was awarded a Pushcart Prize and appeared in *The Pushcart Prize XXIII: The Best of the Small Presses* (1999). "April," "Bird Nests," "Crepuscule," "Rear Window," and "Small Pleasures" were reprinted in *The New Young American Poets* (Southern Illinois University Press, 2000). "The Closer You Get," appeared on *Poetry Daily* (www.poems.com). "After Sleep the Wild Morning" was selected for *The Beacon Best of 2001*. "Small Pleasures" was reprinted in *The Logan House Anthology of 21st Century American Poetry* (2001). "Children in a Field" appeared in *Ted Kooser's American Life in Poetry* column.

I wish to thank the Constance Saltonstall Foundation for the Arts, the Fine Arts Work Center in Provincetown, Massachusetts, and the National Endowment for the Arts for their support. I'm grateful to my teachers and friends who advised and encouraged me as I wrote these poems. Special thanks to Amy Sara Carroll, Kyoko Uchida, Nina Revoyr, Junot Díaz, Nathalie Anderson, Tanya Boudreau, and Dita Andersson Everett. Thanks to my parents, William and Linda Shaw, and to my sister and brother-in-law, Amanda and Mark Milewski. For everything: thank you Felix, Phineas, and Beatrice L'Armand.